Triumphs of the Ordinary Woman

Essays on Reposition Resilience Restoration

Quindola Crowley

authorHOUSE®

AuthorHouse™
1663 Liberty Drive
Bloomington, IN 47403
www.authorhouse.com
Phone: 1-800-839-8640

First published by AuthorHouse 1/24/2011

ISBN: 978-1-4567-1622-6 (sc)
ISBN: 978-1-4567-3322-3 (e)

Library of Congress Control Number: 2011900064

Printed in the United States of America

Any people depicted in stock imagery provided by Thinkstock are models, and such images are being used for illustrative purposes only. Certain stock imagery © Thinkstock.

This book is printed on acid-free paper.

This book is about life, the transitions, and the many struggles that the ordinary woman encounters in a life time. It's about fundamental issues that frame who we are. It's about relationships, health, living, poor choices, and consequences. It's about mothers and daughters. And finally it's all about understanding the power of forgiveness, the transformation that repositioning creates, being resilient and learning that restoration comes in the form of living. This book is about you and me; the women who redefine success, over challenges, and learn to live life on our own terms.

I was able to compile the stories of women counseled; women who attended focus groups and weave them with my own story. This work has been in the making for many years. It is presented to you, so that you may begin the transformation and the healing.

This book gives voice to the women who suffer in silence wondering if they will get through. I want you to know that you can.

Yes you can.

Acknowledgements

I would like to thank my family for allowing me to publish this work. I especially give thanks and honor to my priest, my husband, for being my rock, my champion and my best friend. It is because of his strength that I am able to be strong and do the work that I am commissioned to do. My children are incredible, resilient and phenomenal in all aspects of their being. I honor them with this work because they are living the life as they continue to grow with me and as they stretch themselves. They too have stories of triumph that weave themselves through this life they are present with and the lives of others. My hope for them is that one day they allow for their stories to be a platform for the healing journey of others.

Author Notes

I pray this work resonates with the core of your being. It is my gift to your health and your journey to wholeness. For me it was difficult yet liberating to write this and to allow God to use me. I feel naked and a bit exposed; I have had to go back and edit because some things were difficult to share. However I feel that I have given of myself in such a way that it allows others to understand that secrets have no power when they are exposed -that truth is healing and forgiveness is essential. Faith is everlasting.

Be well, Be Inspired, Give Back

Quindola Crowley

Quindola Crowley
LICSW, BCD, PhD(c)
Minister- Life Coach

Foreward

*W*hen life happens, we can choose to be victimized by it, or be victorious over it. "Triumphs of the Ordinary Woman" is a journal, as well as a type of road map, in moving forward to victory. Ms. Crowley captures the elements in short bursts of insight, while giving the reader a chance to reflect on how best to apply the lessons that grow out of that time of reflection.

As I read and pondered my own life journey against the transitions to victory listed in her book, I found myself rooted in what I knew to be true. Restoration comes to us as we move out in courage, willing to take our position on the edge of our life, without a sense of entitlement, with a deadly and insatiable hunger for the comfortable. Instead, be willing to dig deep into your character and trust that the God who made you is also the God who will keep you through every transition. We can trust that our resilience, coupled with His Grace, is sufficient for all life expericnces.

As I read this book, I knew that it was a gift and a reminder. As you read about the "Triumphs of the Ordinary Woman" , sit with your pencil, a cup of tea, and some good ole' fashion "pondering time". You will probably see yourself in it. You won't be sorry!!

Jeni Gregory
PhD, LICSW
Heartland Counseling
Principal

In addition to Heartland Counseling, Dr. Gregory is internationally recognized as a leading expert on working with children in cross cultural environs. Specific to her expertise is child soldiers impacted with Profound Catastrophic Trauma. She is a specialist in international pediatric traumatology. She has published numerous peer reviewed journal articles and expects "One Love Deep in Africa: Children of War in Recovery" (book) to be published soon.

Contents

" She is a quiet beauty as salty as the sea and as hard as the white crested waves that carry out the novice who never seems to return, so beautiful so calm so inspiring yet like a quiet storm one day she will erupt like a natural disaster...Hurricane Lou please don't destroy me don't destroy us all. Your misty breeze was once my peace, my strength, my solace... like the sparkling sand heated by the warmth of the sun."

On Mothers and Daughters

No book on Triumph could be written without discussing mother/daughter relationships. So often we are defined by our mothers. We are a fusion of who they are because of the strange symbiotic relationships that we carry into our adulthood. We are who they are or who they think we should be even as we try to move out of their shadows and create our own paths.

Sometimes the relationship can be very painful, disturbing and unhealthy. *"In the deep core pit of my being I still feel the pain, the pain of a wounded spirit. Is it my pain or does it belongs to her? I don't know. Pain has so many owners, lovers, companions, friends, enemies and soul mates. Pain is like tired old slippers comfortably worn by the owners of pain."*

Mothers have walls that sometimes shut you out- walls built up and doors that close shut. Mamas have bosoms that comfort, smother, and leave you drunk with scents of sweet security and nurturing. Moms are good friends. *"She is the best mom a daughter could ask for…it has been a long time since I talked to my mom. I wish I could ask her who I am. Am I all or none or one? Who am I? Hey mom I'm over here. Can you see me… yes Mother I'm here."*

It was a tremendous hurdle trying to define myself when I was raised by this mother who was parenting out of the complexities of life. It was difficult stuff that caused me to pause. It puzzles me when I grapple with how difficult and complicated it must have been for my mother to have 3 children by time she was 18, two of which were conceived out of rape and violence. How do we parent from a place of pain? How do you parent and develop a healthy nurturing relationship when you have not had that for yourself and you don't know what it looks like, feels like, or smells like? Better yet how did she parent her daughters when all she knew was wrapped up in her own mother rejecting her and not believing her?

My incredible mother was the contradiction of all that I write about. She is the contradiction that sends one into a tailspin. With all that was going on within her, she somehow created something for me that I could hold on to. Because of what she created for me, I know that love smells like the perfumed bosom of my tired and spent mom when she held me close at the end of the day. I know it smells like my great grandfather "Big Daddy's" musky scent from walking around town on errands and from working in the garden. I know that love taste like my great grandmother, "Madea's" 5 layer pineapple coconut cakes and her pecan pie.

My mother was always working or going to school. We would spend a lot of time with my great grandparents. I remember she would come home at Christmas time with lots of gifts. One Christmas she even brought Santa with her. He was a big burly guy with a sparse white beard and a tight fitting red suit. It was all costume but I had no idea. Madea and Big Daddy had this little artificial silver tree with snow around it. The small little silver sparse tree my grandparents kept up looked like a Charlie brown tree with all those gifts around it. I guess that was mother's way of showing her love.

While I was growing up my mother made some terrible choices that have affected me, impacted me, scared me, and even at one time defined me. Those were the things I had to learn to forgive. I learned that she only gave what she knew to give based on what she had in her at the time. When she knew better she did better.

Because of her choices and the crazy stuff that occurred in our house I wanted my adult life to be different. I wanted to parent differently. I wanted to be a different type of wife. I learned from my mother what to do and what not to do. Or at least I thought I did. At some point I really had to examine how I was parenting my daughters. I had to determine if I had caused them irreparable damage if so what damage I had caused and was it recoverable.

My mother was a control freak. Because of the control my mother imposed in our lives I realized that I was perfectionist. My expectations for myself and for those around me did not allow room for mistakes. Now the question was did my years of trying to be the best (that translate as controlling my world and being better than because of feeling like damaged goods) affect my daughters? Did my years of thriving for excellence affect them? Did my years of feeling less than; because of the rape, the abandonment issues, the failed marriage, did that affect the girls? Did the years when I thought I was strong but was really masking pain and shame have an impact on who they would become? I didn't know what I had done to the girls. But as I examined my relationship with my mother and how for years she had so much emotional control over me and everyone around her I realized I too have some of those traits. Worse yet I was concerned about what I had passed along to my daughters.

I realized that my mother was controlling because she did not have control over the rape, the abuse and the horrible things that had happened to her early in life so she controlled everything and everybody around her. The residual damage for me was being afraid to disappoint her. I made straight A's in school so as not to disappoint her; I graduated early from high school and was academically exceptional so as not to disappoint her. I went to college at age 16 so as not to disappoint her.

The truth of the matter is I hid all my mistakes and bad choices from her so as not to disappoint her. I wanted her to be proud of me because somehow she put her hope in me and I knew it. I lived life finishing the things she started completing her dreams. My life mirrored hers. In many ways I was just like her even in the places within myself that I did not want be like her. I had wanted to be perfect in every way and for many reasons. In turn what I taught my girls was that nothing was ever good enough. I sent the message that what they did was not enough and had to be redone. I sent the message to them that I wanted more from them than they had to give. This was the same message my mother had sent me. It took me a long time to realize this. I think I finally changed the message I had sent my girls but it was long after the self esteem issues had surfaced, after the challenges for them had crept in.

So the question arises as to when do we step away from the shadows of our mothers and become our own person. When do we stop allowing the symbiotic relationship to overtake us? How does one find herself when she is woven into the chaos of complicated relationships? When do I learn who I am separate from who mother is or who my mother wants me to be? It finally happened for me when I looked in the mirror and saw myself and not my mother.

One day I sat and took inventory of who I was. I looked myself in the eye and did not break eye contact until I allowed myself to see the woman standing before me. I examined her from the inside out and then from the outside in. I studied her. It was during this self examination that I came to realize the truths of the being that resided in me. I acknowledged that there were aspects of who I had become that was wounded and broken. I also saw the internal strength that created the gateways for change and the journey for living well. It was during this time that my brow creased in thoughtful self reflection with a desire to understand my mother. It was then that forgiveness crept in. I began the process of forgiving. I forgave her, my mother, for being human. I forgave her for not knowing what to do and how to parent us. I forgave her for being complicated and misunderstood. I just forgave her. Forgiveness is healing.

But that's not the end of the story. The fact of the matter is my mother is the transformational "Triumphant" woman in the story. My mother is the woman who overcame the obstacles and the life challenges. She learned along the way to define life on her own terms. In that she even learned to define and create success. Her success is defined partly by the many accomplishments in her life. She was the first in her family to achieve higher education to include doctoral studies. She even had significant career highs during her career. It is from this definition of Triumph that I get the AHA moments. So today when I frame thoughts of my mother I think of her in terms of her success and her ability to overcome and no longer define her by the struggles.

This brings us back to forgiveness. Redefining and reframing really begins with the conscious choice to forgive. When I choose to forgive my mother I had to take personal inventory of myself and accept the fact that I owned some of my dysfunction. I realized how complex and complicated life gets when it is layered with shame and abuse. When I began to celebrate her success and her ability to redefine herself, to reposition her life, and her ability to create in me a zest for learning, a determination that surpasses tenacity, a will to live beyond where my small dreams could take me, and belief that I could reach more. It gave me joy, unspeakable joy, and peace. You see, I realized in her struggle she gave me the best of who she was. In her struggle she showed me that she was vulnerable and that one can only give out of what she has within her. If it is not in you at the time you cannot give that part of yourself. But with that she showed me life is like a running stream. It is constantly refreshing itself; it wears away the ruble and it's fresh and brand new every day. I've learned that love is unconditional and it last through hurts, pains, and disappointment. Love transcends time.

Letter to My Children

Dear Lovely Ones,

I am stopping by to let you hear my voice in the midst of life. Shh be still and quiet so we can have a fire side chat. I was in my mind visiting my mother and the thoughts of her led me to you. So, I wondered how you all are doing. When I was young I called my mother Hurricane El because she would sometimes sweep in so harshly and abrasively and leave us all broken and damaged by the strong winds of her words. Sometimes I wonder if you have ever compared me to a natural disaster. What I do know is that I have a spent a lot time pursuing. I have pursued dreams, education, career opportunities, and business ventures. I realized that I spent a lot of time away both physically and mentally. I realized that while in my pursuits for excellence and betterment I was not always present. Even when I was there physically I was not always there.

In all this I have learned that life does not stand still; tomorrow will come anyway; and yesterday is history. For you that simply means to live your life like it matters. Live your life with a legacy in mind.

I want to know who you are. More importantly you need to know who you are. Who are you when you think no one is looking. Are you the one that pays it forward and gives even when it isn't requested? Are you the selfless person that is still enough, confident enough, and caring enough to hear the silent cries of the ones around you that sometimes hurt? I just want to know if I instilled that compassion in you that creates a character with worth.

Are you content with being who you are even when you know you need to improve on something? Are you coachable and open to learning. I'd like to hope and believe that you are all these things and more because that is what I tried to shape in you. Your journey will reveal to you the many facets of who you are. Be fully engaged in your journey participate with purposefulness and determination. Allow the most gifted, talented, and blessed to pour into you and then give back expecting nothing in return. Then live as if you have accomplished something great today because you really don't know if tomorrow will arrive. Lastly, hug, touch and tell those closest to you that you love them every day. How much you are loved should be the last thing on your mind when you lay your head down to rest.

Love Mom

"Yesterday was so light so airy past the shadows in the wind. Hard to grab hold and recapture. Tomorrow within reach but colorless scentless shapeless. Today is a wonder yet a wonder.grey and soft blue rainy and sunshine bright .I spoke to my mother today she was tired yet uncomplicated pleasant .I heard smiles in the creases of her word. Just for a moment it felt very gentle just for a moment I felt like I was having a conversation with my mom. "

Daughters

"I'd feel a lot braver if I were not so scared"
Hawkeye Pierce

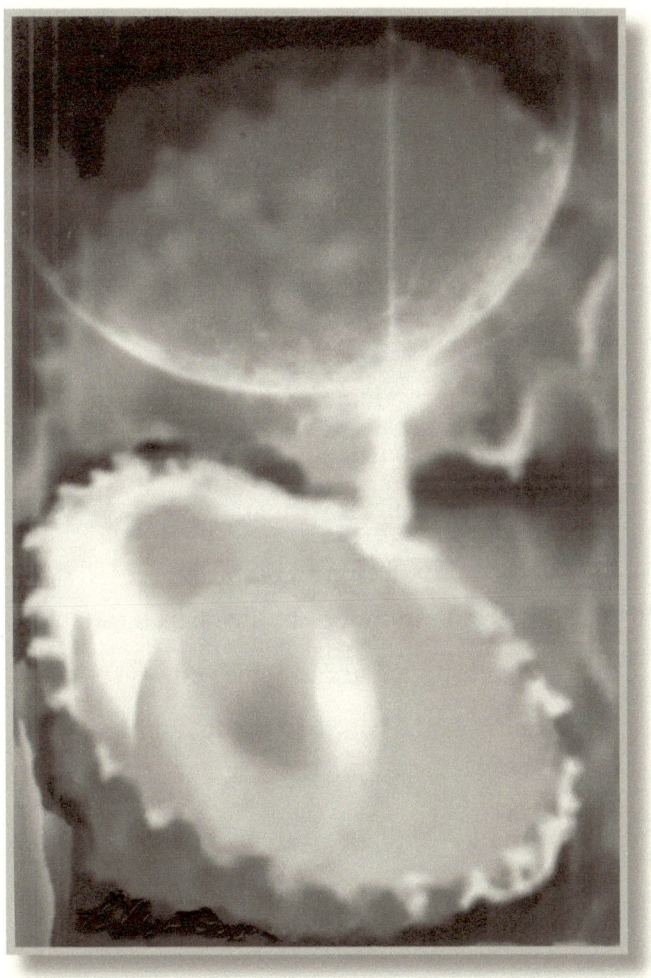

The Kingdom of Heaven is like a merchant looking for fine pearls. When he found one pearl of great value, he went and sold all he had and bought it.
Matthew 13:45

Stevie Leigh

Hey little girl I see you
Young lady… woman… standing tall… proud
green eyes sparkling with life
shy gentle reserved
loud aggressive defensive.
defensive …don't let your guard down,
down is where you will be
keep your head up.
Box em up motions… you know the drills
watch the court and play your game…
of life… life is what you make it
take it and run …drive to the basket and shoot.
Don't be afraid to shoot - in life take all the shots
some you make and some you won't
but won't be your best if you don't try
Drive baby drive
I'm so proud to see that you are living life overcoming
and driving…drive…drive…drive..

Mimi

Don't lose yourself my lady the world is a big place

Searching for a dream

Where is Waldo? I don't know. Who's on first?

Don't get caught up in the do up, be up, act up, wrap it up,

It's your thang do what you want to do

Be black Opal… Punky is a way of life Brewster…

Like diamonds can be raw that's ok

For Us Sisters

Sisters so close

we share the same blood

yet different as night and day.

Both know that together we stand

Am I my sister's keeper?

Her eyes mirror my soul --both wanting, both needing,

both feeling, both searching, both missing the nurturing,

both standing alone in the crowded space
...and still alone we both feel.

yet different as night and day.

Am I my sister's keeper?

Is she her sister's keeper?

Are you your sister's keeper?

Daughter

Last night I cried

Last night I cried for you for your innocence lost

I cried for my little girl

I cried for the young woman standing before me

My tears, my salty tears drip the dreams

of my mother her sisters, my grandmother and my great grandmother.

My tears scented with the sweet memory of a precious little girl

The memory of a head nested in the bosom of love
sweetened by the smell of mommas toiled work day.

My tears didn't just drip quietly they raged and
poured like a storm out of control

Last night I cried. I cried for you

I cried for your innocence lost

Last night I cried

I cried for me too

Personal Reflections

Journal Notes

May my prayer be set before you like incense;
May the lifting up of my hands be like the evening sacrifice
Psalm 141:2

By His Stripes We are Healed

On Health Challenges

I was most inspired by the strength of a woman I did not know but simply had a brief encounter with. This woman clearly took charge of her health and decided she would not allow the health issue to define her. I don't know the process or the journey for Suzette but in our brief encounter I was taken by her amazing will to survive. Suzette and I shared a commercial ride to the airport. As I sat next to her I could feel her and the intensity of her energy. It was gentle yet bold and unwavering and still yet warm. Suzette shared with me that she was traveling to Mexico to undergo alternative treatment for a medical condition. It was a condition she would not name. I suspect that she refused to call it anything because that would somehow validate it. She had a confidence about her that defied the fear and concern that seemed to rest in her belly. It was that confidence and security that gave her Triumph over the illness. It was in that brief encounter that I gained so much from her strength. She had a quiet that bellowed throughout the van in such a powerful, yet gentle, yet confident way. She showed strength to overcome. She had strength and a will to live for herself, a will to live for her grand children. It is short encounters like these that keep me grounded in being present with myself, my family, and my friends. *I have vowed to hear as to be heard to seek to understand so as to be understood. Triumph.*

Sometimes my body hurts and I don't know how to explain why my arm hurts knowing I am not having a heart attack. It is crazy because I go in and no one seems to really understand why I wake up tired or why the bottom of my feet hurt. I hurt in places that don't make sense. All I did was sleep through the night (well not really). I don't sleep well because of the pain.

When you live with chronic fatigue and chronic pain, it is sometimes difficult to focus and to process information. For me it started in my joints. All of my joints hurt. It began in my hip then it went to my knees, then my elbows hurt when I did pushups and now my fingers hurt.

According to the American College of Rheumatology one in 50 Americans have fibromyalgia and between 80 and 90% of those diagnosed with fibromyalgia are women. I was recently diagnosed with fibromyalgia. I have lived with these symptoms for years and could not understand why some days I simply did could not get out of bed and why on some days I awakened as if I have already worked a full day and my back ached. I ached all the way down to the soles of my feet.

I learned to mask the pain. I learned that people are so caught up in their own thing that unless you have some illness that is clearly visible or unless it has a vicious label on it like lupus or cancer no one cares. Chronic health issues are chronic for the person who lives with the experience. For those that interact in your life at some point the problem no longer exits and becomes the norm of how they interact with you. Sometimes this is good and sometimes it means they don't understand how to relate to you. It's funny how people only see what you show them. Or do they only see what they want to see.

Each day I get up and I put on my makeup because if I did not, you would see bags under my eyes. I did not start wearing makeup until I started dealing with chronic pain and fatigue. I realized then that I was covering up. The makeup allowed me to put on my happy face. It allowed me to present to the world what they needed to see.

Because I want to operate in my highest functioning self, I chose to live out life presenting to myself and the world my best. So I force myself up and I force myself out. When I learned about fibromyalgia, I learned that all of my chronic complaints had some validity. I realized that so much of what goes on with me is not in my head. I realized that my body is ultra sensitive to pain. I now had validation to why I felt the things I often feel and how liberating it is to actually know that I'm not a hypochondriac or that I'm not crazy.

The funny thing is I don't often complain. I just smile and keep pressing on. I learned long ago that most often no one cares if you complain too much or that they don't know what to do to help. I don't even talk to my husband about it. He just knows that I'm tired and my legs hurt. My personality doesn't allow me to quit or be still so I get depressed when I get so tired or achy and can't function at the level I'd like to function. I don't want this body to slow me down. I have things to do. However, this is usually when I crash and simply can't go on for a few days. *I have learned to listen to my body.*

I have found that many women are experiencing similar health issues. So I know this is not just my story but its Grace's story, Laina's story, and all the women who are not medically heard and choose to press on. It was Grace who told me how crazy it is for her when she knows that people will ask her foolish questions such as "so what did you do aggravate it"? Not realizing that sometimes there are no explanations. For those that do not suffer from this they don't understand that at times your body responds to the environment or nothing at all. It's interesting how your body can be a barometer for the weather. The fact of the matter is no one really understands that good stress as well as bad stress can exacerbate the flare up of pain. Your body does not know the difference it just reacts. Most often your support group does not understand that even you don't know why there is no explanation as to why today is worse than yesterday and tomorrow who knows. When Grace shared her story she said she gets tired of trying to explain why she is so tired or why she hurts or why she has to pace herself. What is most compelling is that Grace mirrored my own feelings of how she **gets tired of being tired**.

Society is focused on wellness. There are so many wellness programs out there. Everywhere you turn there is new program popping up to address wellness. On some level I know we all want to be physically well and understand that there are prevention measures that we can incorporate in our lives that will help us to be well. What about the stuff that just happens. For years I have been challenged with some idiotic health challenge that was puzzling for me. I have had several major surgeries. One of the surgeries I had is normally reserved for women 65 years or older. I think I was 40 when it happened to me. Then there is the battle with gravity. Gravity grabs hold of the body and literally pulls it down. I personally refuse to allow it govern my lifestyle and make the rules. I refuse to let it win. Such as life.

What concerns me about this wellness issue is how women tend to live in the "strong place" and operate in their issues as if they can handle them all alone. They don't ask for support and often feel alone- afraid to reach out. What about the "strong place". I see that as a placebo for managing the things of life. We take the "strong place" pill and keep on moving telling ourselves that we are ok. As we all know placebos are the proverbial "sugar-pill". It is the medical intervention given in place of the real thing (drug) and those that receive it often report improvement because they believe they have the real thing. The problem with this is that we simply mask the issues that reside with us, while looking down and not reaching out for help. It is in the truest of "strong places" that we are weakest. It is in those strong places where we are most vulnerable. It is in this vulnerable place that the healing begins both physically and mentally. See it is when we expose the problem- take it out of the darkness that the light is able to bring about a renewal of strength.

When I sat down with Joan she talked about how for years she dealt with being bipolar. Joan shared how every day she had to struggle with being present with herself and with her family. She had to work collaboratively with her doctor, who would put together just the right blend of medications that would help her to be coherent. This med cocktail would allow her to be free of the sluggish feeling and the drugged feeling. Joan worked very hard to be alert so she could get up in the morning and make breakfast for the family – get her kids off to school. It was her desire to "Triumph" over the illness that allowed her to be the best advocate for her son who deals with learning disabilities or her youngest child who has attention deficit disorder. Joan was committed to being alert when her six year old was pinging from the walls because she is ADHD. For Joan life success and health success is redefined. She does not define success by the BA degree or the Masters degree she holds, or the successful business she has. Yes these are all great accomplishments. But Joan's success is defined moment by moment by the fact that she can get up each morning and be clear in her thoughts. Being well is relative and for Joan well is when she is clear enough to parent her children, be a good wife to her husband, accomplish the challenges she sets before herself and be a good friend in the midst of it all.

Joan's success is defined by her strength to carry on when she feels no one understands and she has no support. Like she says not many understand what it means to live with mental illness or the challenges of parenting children who have medical issues and require medication to manage their behavior. Joan is Triumphant. I celebrate her.

Personal Reflections

Journal Notes

_____

_____

_____

_____

_____

_____

_____

_____

_____

_____

_____

_____

_____

_____

_____

_____

_____

_____

_____

_____

"I fell into the bowels of yesterday so far that I wasn't sure how to find my way out. The abyss of the bowels of yesterday can consume you to the point of no tomorrow ...no tomorrow. So many women live in the wake of yesterdays mistakes and heartaches. They are unable to see today because their view is clouded by the past."

On Finding Your Way Back

W hen I find myself feeling sorry for myself trying to have a pity party all by myself inviting some but not others you always know who to invite to a pity party. It's the girlfriend that hates life, her husband, her kids, her boyfriend, her job, her hair, her looks, her body, even her nails. I can go on and on but you get the picture. You know the one. She comes and brings the whine- I mean the wine and cheese. She is the greatest energy zapper and oxygen thief you know. How does one rid herself of these types of acquaintances or better yet how does one keep herself from falling into a self pity mode?

Its women like Lou, who carry their pain like medals on their chest. Lou, she, has some prized ones. There are some that I know she is exceptionally proud of. First there is the childhood rape resulting in a child. That medallion is encased in a physical assault and a rape of the soul and of the spirit. Then there is the loss, love lost, and death. Death is draped across her shoulders like a cloak as she wears the grief and longs for the life of a lost child. And then there is the loss of the living child, the child who desires to be near but is pushed away. Big medals are pinned to her lapel and hang boldly and close to her chest. This awesome pain is to be revered, chronic cancerous to be held and displayed like trophies in a proud me case. Lou wears pain that clouds the soul and spirit and does not allow for movement or repositioning. This type of pain doesn't allow love, grace, or mercy to temper the spirit and soothe the soul. This type of pain isolates and feeds on itself. I feel sad for Lou and I pray that one day the windows of her soul will open up and a fresh new anointing will pour into her a deliverance from all that torments her. Like Lou so many women are draped in the in the pains of the past. They wear those pains like comfortable throws while they sit and rock alone in the night. By day they robe themselves in anger and mistrust. Because they live in the bowels of toxic mistrust, un-forgiveness, shame, guilt and whatever they can't breathe. In their world is dark even though there is sun beyond the clouds. In their world it's hard to find the fresh air. They have worn the pain so long they do not know how to reposition.

It takes a person like Flo to share a story of Triumph that allows us to see life beyond the grey clouds. Flo said she spent years in the wilderness. For Flo it was a 30 year journey to being well and being whole. She said, "I learned to celebrate along the way. I learned to thank God for journey and I learned that no matter what you encounter you can get through it. The key is staying engaged in life. If you disengage from life you get depressed. This is what happened to Lou. She disengaged and got lost in her darkness.

Then there was Carla with the many accomplishments: college graduate decorated and accomplished military officer. It was Carla who so very clearly shared the fact that we often show people what we them to see. She said no one really knows who she is. People see the accomplishments from the outside. Carla explained that, "the real accomplishment comes when I learned to accept myself and learn to love myself." She went on to say, "I have to learn to validate myself and I am still evolving. I came from a hard life and no one really knows that I experienced drug addiction or homelessness as a young child with my mom. No one really knows my journey has been one of hard times and difficulties. So for me the journey continues and I realize now where my strength lies. I realized that God has always kept me even when I did not know He was there. Yet I am still in the journey."

Grace smiled a lot and said I am simply blessed. She said going back to school and getting a Masters degree was quite an accomplishment. She struggles with physical limitations and challenges that slow her down. But she said the good thing is I never quit. I celebrate everyday with prayer by loving life. I have learned to look up, to stop and smell the roses.

Grace a very courageous woman of Triumph said her greatest

accomplishment was learning not to live in the broken places. Reconciling the crazy stuff and learning to forgive. She said you have to be strong in the broken places. Life is not about finding yourself (unless you are truly lost) it is more about creating yourself.

Just how does one learn not to live in the broken places? How does one learn to embrace the best of who you are while sitting in the valley? After working with many women and dealing with my own issues I have learned that meditating on past hurts gives us permission to assume the life of a victim. As victims we embrace our worthlessness and we transcend that same worthlessness to our daughters. Even when we try to disguise the victimization with denial, or escape it often manifest itself in how treat ourselves, the choices we make and the unhealthy relationships we have.

At some point in your life you have to reposition yourself from victim to victor. You must claim the victory over the healing in your body, the healing of your soul, and request the peace of mind that you desire. The request comes in the form of asking for strength, for salvation and for deliverance. *Lord at this time I pray a quiet prayer for strength. Lord and I look up to you for restoration. I ask that my body be healed, my faith be restored and that you create in me a resilience that pushes me past the difficulties and allows me to be whole even in the broken places.*

Personal Reflections

Journal Notes

Listen to my prayer, O God, do not ignore me.
My thoughts trouble me and I am distraught.
I cast my cares on the Lord He will sustain me

Psalm 55

On Life's Milestones

They Create Opportunities for Growth

I guess I can start with graduating high school at age 16, as the valedictorian and heading off to college with honors. I'm sure that sets the tone for something great. Well I soon learned that I wasn't as smart as I thought, Boy was I naïve. The year I went off to college I really thought that I was grown. "I'm grown", I'd say to my mother. Since I'm grown, I'm going to a college dance alone (mainly because my best friend could not go with me). That night I was raped by the guy I had walk me to my car. He forced me into my car and had me drive into the projects across the street from the university and raped me. I still remember his eyes as he looked at me while I pleaded for him to stop.

Sometimes I remember the smell of his clothes as he forced my head to his lap. Then there are things I have no recollection of at all. I don't remember how I drove home that night with my pants still at my ankles. I don't remember anything about the hospital visit or the faces of the staff. This defining moment changed the course of my life. That experience shook me to the core of my soul. I did not know how to recapture my innocence, my precociousness, the zest for life (milestone). I went away to basic training about 6 months later. Sure it helped to restore my confidence. I came back with a new false sense of pride and self assurance. This confidence helped me band aid some things and get through. I made it through ROTC at University of Houston and then prior to getting commissioned as a 2nd Lt. I found myself pregnant and not married. This almost cost me my commission. Milestone and learning point here. These are choices that change the course of life. I realized then that my decisions had consequence. I never thought those things through prior to that.

This was just the beginning. Life would throw curve balls, lemons and rocks. I think it was the rocks that helped me to change. The rocks hurt. But because I had a strong will I realized that I was not a quitter. Adversity made me try harder; a no propelled me to push until I got a yes or proved them differently. I never gave up. If one door closed I would go knock on another door. Actually, I would spend some time trying to break open the closed door until I realized I needed to move on.

Opportunities for growth are often termed mistakes by others but I see those mistakes or poor decisions as opportunities. When we make bad choices or mistakes we have the opportunity to learn from it and then do better. There are teaching moments in every consequence of life's choices. I know this stuff is easier said than done but I lived it. I have been called Polly Anna with the positive attitude. Always thinking and knowing, hoping that tomorrow will be better. And then since today is not over I still have time to do better. I still have time to make a difference. I think realizing that change is the main constant in life and with change comes opportunities was the revelation that opened the doors of significance. Significance come when you understand that like the flowing waters of a fresh brook so are you. You need to be constantly refreshing yourself and as the strong waters refresh, cleanse, and renew it also reshapes the path by gently and timelessly eroding the matter that was in the way.

Milestone – I was about 27 years old when I went back to grad school. It was then I entered the social work program at University of Illinois. By then I had done some compelling things in my life to work toward my own healing even though I did not fully understand it. I had worked as a rape crisis advocate, counselor. I chaired the speaker's bureau giving talks on sexual assault. I even went into the elementary schools and taught CAP child assault prevention. That's where every child learned that Uncle Harry had no power and if he touched you inappropriately it was ok to tell someone.

So here I am sitting in a psychology class. The class gets all caught up in the discussion. It was then I felt as though I had an out of body experience. The discussion was about me. I saw myself in the text. There I was in black and white between the pages interspaced between victims and victors, with symptoms, and disorders. It was a startling revelation that caused me to seek out professional help. It was then that I realized I needed to deal with my own issues. I learned that I wasn't crazy but I sure had allowed those life challenges to dictate the future and permeate my presence (present). I had shaped my worth around the lies in my head. It was then that I learned I had issue with my mother. The counselor had to tell me. Of course it's always the mothers fault. But this was a classic case of something. I don't know if I want to label it.

Consider the milestones in your life. The key point here is to allow yourself the AHA moment. The AHA moment allows you to discover who you are and why you are? What are the pivotal moments that changed the course of your life? What are key events that shaped you? Are these the events that drive your behavior, your choices, and your perceptions of others? Is it one of those pivotal events that shape the way you manage relationships in your life? Just how do you interact with those pivotal times when the memories present themselves? Are you still wounded by them? Does your heart race, palms sweat and do you feel anxious when you think of that pivotal time in your life.

Take a personal inventory and journey into the mind of yourself and discover who resides there. Who are you really? Go beyond the person that the world is allowed to see. Go beyond the person that others see. Go into the shadows of your mind and find the person that hides in the closet. Find the person that no one is allowed to see. Bring that side of you to the light. Have the real you illuminated so that you can see who you are. Sit down with yourself and take inventory of your life and discover the inner workings of this person you live with.

Once you get that inventory sheet complete evaluate it for success. If you look closely you will see that those pivotal moments grew you. Daily life presents us with opportunities for growth. There may be times we miss the lesson and end up getting a redo. That simply means we need to go over the lesson again. When you have the insight to recognize that you have traveled that road before its then that you are well on the way to changing the course of your life. I could spend a lot of time talking about the milestones in my life that caused opportunities for me to grow. I feel it is important to put life in perspective when we define success, balance, life, and living well. It's important to put these life challenges in perspective when we talk about overcoming and hurdling mountains, breaking down walls, getting the breakthrough and living a life of Triumph.

Truly, in the mean time I have learned to operate in my strengths, to choose wisely how to spend my time. Yes, sometimes I over commit. I do that because sometimes it is what gets me out of bed. Yet for the most part my actions and interactions are intentional and very purposeful. I analyze often the short as well as the long term plan. I ask the question-Does what I'm doing right now take me where I need to go or am I spending time in a place I don't belong? This especially matters if you are working a job as cook when you really want to teach preschool. It is critical for your healing and your well-being that you do a self assessment of where you are and where you want to go. Allow it to take shape, and then create a road map of the process. Get on that road to success and triumph. Understand that pit stops along the way are okay and that you have the power to change the course. The key is in knowing where you want to go and where you are going so you can work toward getting there. That is working with purpose on purpose.

Personal Reflections

Journal Notes

_____

_____

_____

_____

_____

_____

_____

_____

_____

_____

_____

_____

_____

_____

_____

_____

_____

You are about to cross the Jordan to enter and take possession
of the land the Lord your God is giving you. When you have
taken it over and you are living there, be sure you obey all
the decrees and laws I am setting before you this day.

Deuteronomy 11:31

On Repositioning

My journey has shown me that my words are inspired by pain… my pain…her pain, our pain. Remarkably so I don't hurt like that anymore. Thank God. I really mean it thank God .My heart does not pour out grievous body shaking tears any longer. My pain is more like a dull sharpness that occasional pierces me. It is the kind of pain that surprises you once in a while like the pain of an old wound scared over and mostly healed. If you touch it gently or make a sudden movement a sensation jars the memory and a sharp pain arises yet is easily forgotten as one continues to move. It's like the pain in your back that you feel while you are sleeping. As you roll into that feeling you can remember the epidural from that first child but the pain is fleeting because as you reposition the pain goes away. The good thing is that that sharp pain comes only long enough to remind you of the healing and then it is easily forgotten as one continues to reposition.

Repositioning is critical. One has to reposition herself to rid herself of the pain of yesterdays hurts. Repositioning and reinventing as you move through life. Repositioning is about living in a place of forgiveness and healing. The forgiveness is the healing that allows the scars to soften and to not be so tender to the touch. Some scars are very painful. These scars are often large and portentous. They are very ugly and we try to hide them with makeup –work success, alcohol, food, shopping, or sex but they still hurt.

I was able to reposition to the place of forgiveness. I like this place of gentle forgiveness because it has allows my soul to breathe- to be uncluttered. My basket is light and not over burdened with other people's stuff. I am referring to stuff I don't need to carry around with me, stuff that slows your movement and makes you sluggish, stuff that tempers your grace with anger and resentment, stuff that smolders and aches chronically. You know the stuff that requires constant medication. I realized that I don't hurt like that any longer.

Repositioning means to be strong in the broken places. To reposition is to be able to see life for what it is, to accept it, to own your part of it, and to move on. You have to accept the things that have been done, understand that they can't be undone. Joann can't change the fact that her marriage is over and the divorce is final. She can't change the fact that her children won't have the two parent home that she so desired. What she can change is how she chooses to move forward. Take inventory on what you have learned from the experience. Then make a conscious choice to live in the excellence of who you are rather than the broken person life tried to make you out to be. I call it the "so what life happens" attitude.

Yes this is the point where you just say to yourself ok "**so what**". All the crap in the world has been dumped in your lap and you don't know how to clean yourself up and make your life relevant. You begin by saying "**so what**". So what if you were raped and abused, so what if Uncle Joe molested you. So what if your husband left you with three kids, so what if you were homeless, on drugs, beaten. **So what**! For those of you that did not experience that type of trauma your so what comes in the form of overcoming work issues, promotions, being looked over and passed over. Your life is relevant and what you have to contribute is relevant. And by the way you have triumphed by just staying alive and pushing past the crazy.

Stop allowing what happened in your past life to cloud your future. Of course those significant events were relevant enough to be a placeholder in your life; however they are not relevant enough to define you. If you give that stuff too much power it overcomes you and takes over. You have the opportunity to reshape your life with significance. You have the opportunity to decide right now that no longer will the shame of the past, the hurts of yesterday, and mishaps of life shape your future.

Repositioning requires you to change how you focus on life. Focus on living rather than dying. Focus on being well rather than being sick; Focus on what really matters – did you put too much sand in the jar and is there enough room for the large rocks- the large rocks are the really important things in life. The bottom line is how you spend your time and energy determines the wrinkles in your brow, the gray in your hair and the acid in your stomach. If you succumb to the disasters of life then life will be a disaster.

So how did I arrive at peace and begin the journey. I don't know that I have actually arrived. What I do know is that it is definitely a journey and not a destination. Peace begins with forgiveness and acceptance. We often misunderstand the reason for forgiveness. Often times we think that if we forgive someone it frees them from what they have done to us. It is the exact opposite. Forgiveness liberates us from the shackles of hurt, pain, anger and whatever else it is that keeps us bound up.

In order to begin the journey of forgiveness one must first make a choice to forgive. At this point understand that the hurt does not suddenly disappear nor does the pain but in your mind you have made a choice. Forgiveness is a journey. My understanding is that God forgives us on a daily basis even though we create pain, anger and hurt in the lives of ourselves and others. Making the choice to forgive is the first step in the journey. Real forgiveness involves understanding the hurt or the issue. So the next step is to understand who owns the cause of the hurt. If Uncle Joe molested you when you were 12 what responsibility did you as a child bear in the vicious trauma? I would submit to you that you as a child bear no responsibility. The adult in the situation owns it all. Now that you know who owns the responsibility for the cause of the pain. Now you should "**interview your anger**". Interview your anger and try to understand who associates with the anger. Does your anger hang out with shame, guilt, insecurity, or some other mask? Does your anger position itself in your life as a treasure that sits on the mantle near your heart? Interview your anger and get to know who it is and why it is.

Once you really understand why you are angry you can start owning forgiveness. Forgiveness is for you. Why are you angry? Are you angry with yourself? Why are you angry with yourself? If your marriage dissolved because your husband was violent or was a cheater that does not mean you could have done anything differently or been better in any way. It simply means that choices were made that were not healthy for your relationship. He participated it those choices and he owns them. And then again what if it was that complicated or messy but just didn't work out. Perhaps you were the one that was a mess and caused the relationship to end. Perhaps you are like Marla who does not feel good about her choice of partners because she is still waiting for her first love to get his act together and no one else can match up. She sabotages every relationship because she maintains an unhealthy desire to go backwards to the fantasy of what could be. You have to own your stuff. "**Interview the anger and inventory the baggage.**"

What you own are the choices you make for yourself. You own the choice to choose life and to learn from those pivotal moments in your life. You own the choice to forgive yourself. Sometimes we have to forgive ourselves for being human, for feeling, for loving too much and even for being insecure. Sometimes we need to forgive ourselves for making the choices we made. We learn that we made choices based on what we knew at that time.

Once you interview your anger take inventory of all the baggage that sits in the closets of your mind. Take inventory of the emotions that have saddled you with setbacks. Write a list and put it on paper. Sitting down and putting things on paper is a powerful tool that allows you see the real you. It pulls that stuff from inside of you and puts it out there so you can do something with it. Often times we keep our stuff all bottled up inside and we don't know what to do with it. Once you take it outside by writing it down it allows you to see it for what it is. At this point you can do something with it. You have the power to confront it, to examine it and the power to even throw it away.

Your destiny with peace is determined by the worth you see in yourself. Of course for me it has always been a God thing. My worth was determined long ago by the price paid on the cross. Of course I would not have turned my child over to save the life of anyone but that was the price paid for me so I know my worth is greater. And my latter shall be greater. Your latter shall be greater.

Peace is a position of power in life. You can reposition for power and for peace. When you realize that nothing from the past has power over you there will be peace. If you unmask today and reposition yourself-your life can be changed. You have the power to choose change and have life everlasting.

The woman that is able to reposition herself is measured based on her ability to overcome adversity. It is not just in the overcoming but in the manner in which she overcomes. Does she scream and shout and pout her way through or does she move gracefully through trials with praise and faith. I personally have done it all but at some point there should be less screaming and pouting and more praising and stronger faith. It is the faith that allows us to move gracefully through knowing that we shall Triumph.

Personal Reflections

Journal notes

_____

_____

_____

_____

_____

_____

_____

_____

_____

_____

_____

_____

_____

_____

_____

_____

_____

I remember when I was little I used to lay in the front yard and look into the night sky. Whenever you look into the sky at night you will always see at least one star even if there are clouds in the sky. That only means that you have to look harder for the star. I believe that as long as I can see a burning star in the sky, then there will always be hope. Hope for a better tomorrow, hope to get closer to my dreams, and hope to succeed.

Alex 2009

On Restoration

*O*f all the women I have encountered I wondered what got them through. When I asked what defined success in their lives they came back with thoughts on being resilient. They came back with simple things like mastering grandma's recipe. Gloria said it was important to her to be able to bake the bread and create the smell in the house she recalled from her childhood. She wanted to recreate the sense of strength and security, the sense of belonging and family that she felt when she sat in the kitchen with her grandmother as she made rolls. It didn't matter that Gloria was a CEO of a very successful company what mattered most to Gloria and how she defined triumph was her ability to create memories and tradition for her children. Gloria wanted for her own children to feel loved each time she made homemade rolls. It wasn't just Gloria that realized that she could not be measured by the countless accolades that the world had given her but by the small measure of truths that filled her soul with peace.

Restoration and peace come with setting priorities. One way we set priorities is by establishing what is important to us and spending our time purposefully. Let's talk about balance for a minute. You have to strike a balance in life. One defines that by their lifestyle. Don't be too busy to be present with life today. Don't be so busy pursuing tomorrow's goals that you miss out on what is happening around you. For instance, don't get so busy looking for a new job that you are not being effective at your current job. Don't be so engaged with the pursuit of additional education that you miss out on the learning and life lessons that are in front you. Creating balance means establishing priorities. If God is a priority in your life then you must spend time nurturing that relationship. If your spouse and your children are a priority, then you spend time developing and nurturing those relationships. How often do we say one thing is a priority in life, but spend most of our time doing something else?

As a minister and life coach, I have spent so much time working in venues and opportunities to empower others that I lost sight of my son. My son had to go through a crisis for me to see him. Not only was I not balanced, I was not living out the priorities that I had set for my life with my family being first. I was not present when I was home. I was either tired, or working on something. None of my time was being spent mentoring, coaching, parenting my son and he surely let me know in a very profound manner. I was hurt and wounded, but I realized that life had taken over. I have learned that life is shorter than we realize, that tomorrow is not promised. You have to have purposeful interactions in life. I see time as a commodity. It is precious, fleeting, and stands still for no one. It can't be bought back or recaptured. If I miss a basketball game I won't see him drive and dunk the way he did in that game. I missed it. I can't recapture that moment. Establish life priorities, make some sacrifice and invest your time where you want the most dividends. Sometimes that means giving up something. Live purposefully.

When I return home from a week on the road, will I spend my Saturday, socially networking (at the approved planned social event) or will I spend my time bowling with my son? You guessed it. I'd go bowling my son because at the end of the day my accomplishments mean nothing if I failed my son and my family.

While explaining the journey to personal restoration I feel compelled to speak about Savanna. Savanna has always been loving and compelling. Savanna is beautiful and complicated. Savanna was beaten with the life (literally) choked out of her. She says her "last breath" cried out Lord. Stevie is a beautiful tortured soul that does not understand her worth, see her beauty or value the skin she lives in. Savannah gets caught up...; external beauty defines her and everyone around her. Savanna lives for the moment and losses sight of life- if it's not in front of her. I think when Savanna is able to truly see herself as God sees her she will know her worth.

I did not speak much about the men in our lives that temper who we are -how we see ourselves and their impact on how we define the exceptions in life. Marla is real confused about the men in her life. It could be because of what her mother taught her. It could be because her father was not there or the father she knew sent mixed messages or it could be... It could be because he was too drunk to talk to her when she was a child... She will then count the journey to wellness as a milestone that continues to propel her in the quest for being whole and complete. Sometimes forgiveness is rekindling relationship and getting to know someone that left you early on because your latter is greater. Forgiveness...

Personal Reflections

Journal Notes

Read Reflect Respond Rest

*W*hat really resonated to me among all these women of courage – these incredible triumphant women was the DNA that flowed between them all. There was something core and fundamental that they all shared. The DNA of triumphant women is their relationship with God. I found that these women, no matter where in the journey, at some pointed reached up and called upon the Lord.

It was Carla who said that even when she did not know God she knew that He kept her. She felt that even in her darkest places that God was keeping watch over her. It was this faith that pulled her out of those dark places- it was this faith that made her look up when there was nothing else for her to grab hold of. It was this faith that has brought her through homelessness, and made her successful in her endeavors. It is this faith that helps her to see that she is worthy and in her journey there is love and acceptance. It is this faith that mirrors the strength that she bestows and the resilience that she has.

As a woman of faith I have found that putting God first means having a strong prayer, meditation, and study life. To be strong in the Lord means to read the word as well as meditate on the word. I **read** and I seek understanding. It was some time before the word resonated with me. It took me a long time to understand how Naomi's life was relevant to mine or that what Abraham experienced meant anything in my life. I prayed for clarity and understanding. I prayed that the Lord would make His word clear and relevant to me. In that prayer time I was able to **reflect** on what I had read. It's in reflection that I was able to make sense of what Paul meant when he said he does the things that he hates. I know that I struggle with the tapes in my head that say I'm not good enough, smart enough, or strong enough. Each day I bring those thoughts into captivity by mediating and **responding** to the truth that resides in me.

The truth of the matter is that I serve a God who loves me. The God I serve wants me to love Him with my whole heart. In doing that I **rest** in peace and I have joy. I have joy in the midst of the storm. Better yet I dance in the rain while it's storming because I know that the storm will pass.

Personal Reflections

Journal Notes

_____

_____

_____

_____

_____

_____

_____

_____

_____

_____

_____

_____

_____

_____

_____

_____

_____

_____

Cover Design

$\mathcal{E}$ laine Nicholas currently lives in Hawaii with her family, She is not defined by pain or labels, but chooses to use her past as a stepping stone to help others find their way. Elaine is a photographer, graphics designer, and currently works as a case manager for those with mental illness. She has three children and despite the clamoring of such children, refuses to add pets to the chaos.

Art Work

Evonne Corvin is a certified psycho educational therapist, and served as Minister of Music before the Lord led her to discover art. Evonne resides in Olympia, Washington, working as a private music and art teacher. She has been married thirty years, and has two adult children. Evonne is devoted to her family life. She began painting with her children during home school lessons in science. From microscope paintings to larger works, Evonne explored varying techniques. After overcoming serious illness, Evonne returned to painting. The artwork has become an outpouring Evonne's love for the Lord and her devotion to prayer life. Evonne's works is captured throughout the pages of this book. I f you would like more information on Evonne's work she can be reached on her website. http://www.freewebs.com/justapeekartwork/